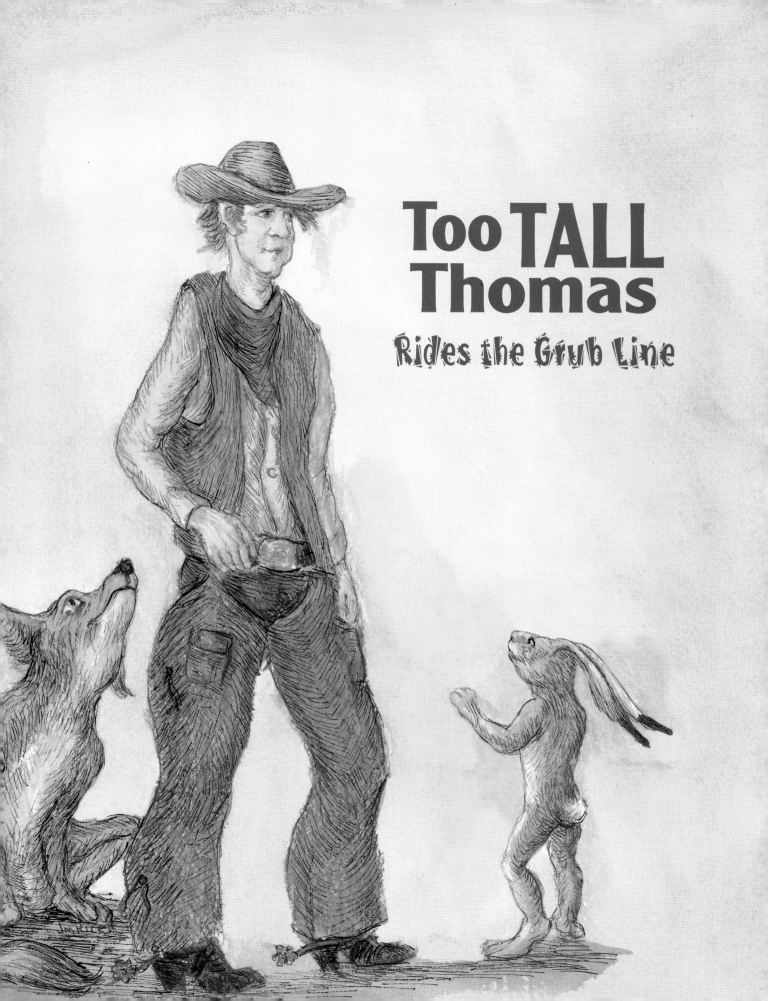

Too TALL Thomas

Rides the Grub Line

**Written and illustrated by
James Rice**

PELICAN PUBLISHING COMPANY
Gretna 2004

The word "Pelican" and the depiction of a pelican are trademarks
of Pelican Publishing Company, Inc., and are registered
in the U.S. Patent and Trademark Office.

Library of Congress Cataloging-in-Publication Data

Rice, James.
    Too Tall Thomas rides the grub line / written and illustrated by James Rice.
        p. cm.
Summary: When Too Tall Thomas finishes the trail drive, he finds miscellaneous
work in exchange for meals, but he cannot wait to get back to real cowboy work.
    ISBN 1-58980-177-6 (hardcover : alk. paper)
    [1. Cowboys—Fiction.] I. Title.
 PZ7 .R3634 To 2004
 [E] —dc22
                                                            2003018921

Printed in China

Published by Pelican Publishing Company, Inc.
1000 Burmaster Street, Gretna, Louisiana 70053

TOO TALL THOMAS RIDES THE GRUB LINE

After the trail drive, a cowboy was faced with a long ride home. It was customary for the ranches along the route to take care of any drifting cowboy. There was always a meal and a bunk available, in exchange for the latest gossip and a day or two of work. Going from ranch to ranch for handouts was called riding the grub line.

The trail drive was over and the money spent. Now it was time for Too Tall Thomas to ride the grub line south.

The first ranch offered beans and bed for fence repairs.

Too Tall Thomas grumbled, "This ain't no kind of work for a cowboy."

He finished the job and rode south.

The next ranch gave him fatback and cornbread to weed the winter garden.

Too Tall Thomas griped as he chopped the weeds.
"This sure ain't no kind of work for a cowboy."
He ambled southward.

The trail led to another ranch,
where he was offered bacon and
eggs to repair the barn roof.

Too Tall Thomas complained as he nailed shingles on
the roof. "I'll be danged if this is fittin' work for a cowboy!"
He was glad to get off the roof and push south.

The next ranch was the pits—clean out the well for
hardtack and jerky. Ridin' the grub line didn't leave
much choice.

Too Tall Thomas fussed as he shoveled dirt and slush from the well bottom. "I'll sure be glad when I can get back to comboyin'!"

He cleaned out the well and shuffled southways.

Another ranch wasn't much better—patch up the leather-
works for biscuits and gravy and a nap in the barn.

Too Tall Thomas fumed, "This is better, but it still ain't proper work for a cowboy!"

He crossed the Texas border and kept his nose pointed south.

Somewhere deep in West Texas, a ranch foreman said, "You can round up strays on the north range. It'll mean all winter in the saddle—beans, bacon, and coffee three meals a day, no roof, no bed, and only a herd of stinkin' cows and a horse for company."

Too Tall Thomas smiled and said, "Now this is fittin' work for a cowboy!"